*Give me but one
hour of Scotland,
Let me see it
ere I die.*

IN PRAISE OF
SCOTLAND

IN PRAISE OF SCOTLAND

Summersdale Publishers Ltd
46 West Street
Chichester
West Sussex
PO19 1RP
UK

www.summersdale.com

Printed and bound in the Czech Republic

ISBN: 978-1-84953-560-1

Substantial discounts on bulk quantities of Summersdale books are available to corporations, professional associations and other organisations. For details contact Nicky Douglas by telephone: +44 (0) 1243 756902, fax: +44 (0) 1243 786300 or email: nicky@summersdale.com.

IN PRAISE OF SCOTLAND

Paul Harper

summersdale

Give me but one
hour of Scotland,
Let me see it ere I die.

WILLIAM EDMONDSTOUNE AYTOUN,
FROM 'CHARLES EDWARD AT VERSAILLES ON
THE ANNIVERSARY OF CULLODEN'

Now the summer's in prime
Wi' the flowers richly blooming,
And the wild mountain thyme
A' the moorlands perfuming.
To own dear native scenes
Let us journey together,
Where glad innocence reigns
'Mang the braes o' Balquhither.

ROBERT TANNAHILL,
FROM 'THE BRAES O' BALQUHITHER'

A record of representative men from among engineers, ironmasters, coalmasters, ironfounders, shipbuilders, shipowners, shipbrokers, bankers, merchants, clergymen, lawyers, medical men, principal and professors of the University, cotton spinners, calico printers, manufacturers; cotton, corn, yarn, sugar, timber, and tobacco merchants; drapery, linen, and chemical manufacturers; brewers, builders, accountants, stock brokers, marine and life insurance agents, philanthropists, architects, civil engineers, journalists, dyers, publishers, stationers, teachers, men of letters, portrait painters, sheriffs, and chamberlains.

JAMES MACLEHOSE, *MEMOIRS AND PORTRAITS OF ONE HUNDRED GLASGOW MEN*

Did not strong connections draw me elsewhere, I believe Scotland would be the country I should choose to spend the remainder of my days in.

BENJAMIN FRANKLIN

Scotland lived, she could never die, the land would outlast them all.

LEWIS GRASSIC GIBBON, *SUNSET SONG*

We had an excellent supper – fresh salmon, a fowl, gooseberries and cream, and potatoes; good beds; and the next morning boiled milk and bread, and were only charged seven shillings and sixpence for the whole – horse, liquor, supper, and the two breakfasts. We thought they had made a mistake, and told them so – for it was only just half as much as we had paid the day before at Dalmally, the case being that Dalmally is in the main road of the tourists. The landlady insisted on my bringing away a little cup instead of our tin can, which she told me had been taken from the car by some children: we set no little value on this cup as a memorial of the good woman's honesty and kindness.

DOROTHY WORDSWORTH, *RECOLLECTIONS OF A TOUR MADE IN SCOTLAND, AD 1803*

O Caledonia! stern and wild,
Meet nurse for a poetic child!
Land of brown heath and shaggy wood,
Land of the mountain and the flood,
Land of my sires! what mortal hand
Can e'er untie the filial band,
That knits me to thy rugged strand!

WALTER SCOTT,
FROM 'THE LAY OF THE LAST MINSTREL'

The mark of a Scot of all classes [is that] he... remembers and cherishes the memory of his forebears, good or bad; and there burns alive in him a sense of identity with the dead even to the twentieth generation.

ROBERT LOUIS STEVENSON,
WEIR OF HERMISTON

Let anyone with an ordinary share of the observing faculty sail round the west coast of Scotland and take note of the successive mountain groups which pass before him and he will acknowledge that the voyage of a couple of hundred miles has been almost as instructive to him as if he had scoured over half the globe... Nowhere in Europe does colour come more notably forward in landscape than in the west of Scotland.

ARCHIBALD GEIKIE, *SCOTTISH MOUNTAINS*

The shout of the welder in the din of the great Clyde shipyards; the speak of the Mearns with its soul in the land; the discourse of the Enlightenment, when Edinburgh and Glasgow were a light held to the intellectual life of Europe; the wild cry of the pipes; and back to the distant noise of the battles of Bruce and Wallace.

DONALD DEWAR, AT THE OPENING OF THE SCOTTISH PARLIAMENT

On the heights of Killiecrankie
Yester-morn our army lay:
Slowly rose the mist in columns
From the river's broken way;
Hoarsely roared the swollen torrent,
And the Pass was wrapped in gloom,
When the clansmen rose together
From their lair amidst the broom.
Then we belted on our tartans,
And our bonnets down we drew,
And we felt our broadswords' edges,
And we proved them keen and true;
And we prayed the prayer of soldiers,
And we cried the gathering-cry,
And we clasped the hands of kinsmen,
And we swore to do or die!

**WILLIAM EDMONDSTOUNE AYTOUN,
FROM 'THE BURIAL MARCH OF DUNDEE'**

O fair the lightly sprinkled waste,
O'er which a laughing shower has raced!
O fair the April shoots!
O fair the woods on summer days,
While a blue hyacinthine haze
Is dreaming round the roots!
In thee, O city! I discern
Another beauty, sad and stern.

Draw thy fierce streams of blinding ore,
  Smite on a thousand anvils, roar
    Down to the harbour-bars;
  Smoulder in smoky sunsets, flare
On rainy nights, while street and square
    Lie empty to the stars.
  From terrace proud to alley base,
  I know thee as my mother's face.

ALEXANDER SMITH, FROM 'GLASGOW'

Beer does not taste like itself unless it is chasing a dram of neat whisky down the gullet – preferably two drams.

COMPTON MACKENZIE

I look upon Switzerland as an inferior sort of Scotland.

SYDNEY SMITH

That most wonderful object of domestic art called Scottish trifle with its charming confusion of cream and cake and almonds and jam and jelly and wine and cinnamon and froth.

OLIVER WENDELL HOLMES JR

Assuredly we must cut our coat to suit our cloth – and the cloth is the tartan.

WENDY WOOD

And though I think I would rather die elsewhere, yet in my heart of hearts I long to be buried among good Scots clods. I will say it fairly, it grows on me with every year: there are no stars so lovely as Edinburgh streetlamps. When I forget thee, auld Reekie, may my right hand forget its cunning!

ROBERT LOUIS STEVENSON,
THE SILVERADO SQUATTERS

There is scarcely any earthly object that gives me more – I don't know if I should call it pleasure, but something which exalts me – than to walk in the sheltered side of a wood or high plantation, in a cloudy winter day, and hear a stormy wind howling among the trees and raving o'er the plain.

ROBERT BURNS

There's a saying in Fife, 'Ah ken her faither,' I knew her father. It means don't get above yourself, we know where you come from.

VAL MCDERMID

The twinkling Earn, like a
blade in the snow,
The low hills scalloped against the high,
The high hills leaping upon the low,
And the amber wine in the cup of the sky,
With the white world creaming over the rim,
She watched; and a keen aroma rose,
Embodied, a star above the snows.

JOHN DAVIDSON, FROM 'WINTER IN
STRATHEARN'

Whaur's yer Wully Shakespeare noo?

SHOUTED BY AN ANONYMOUS SCOT AT
THE FIRST PERFORMANCE OF THE
PLAY *DOUGLAS* BY JOHN HOME

On my lonely walks I have often thought how fine it would be to have the company of Burns. And indeed he was always with me, for I had him in my heart... Wherever a Scotsman goes, there goes Burns. His grand whole, catholic soul squares with the good of all; therefore we find him in everything, everywhere.

JOHN MUIR ON ROBERT BURNS

By lone St Mary's silent lake:
Thou know'st it well, – nor fen nor sedge
Pollute the pure lake's crystal edge;
Abrupt and sheer, the mountains sink
At once upon the level brink;
And just a trace of silver sand
Marks where the water meets the land.
Far in the mirror, bright and blue,
Each hill's huge outline you may view;
Shaggy with heath, but lonely bare,
Nor tree, nor bush, nor brake, is there,
Save where, of land, yon slender line
Bears thwart the lake the scatter'd pine.
Yet even this nakedness has power,
And aids the feeling of the hour:

Nor thicket, dell, nor copse you spy,
Where living thing concealed might lie;
Nor point, retiring, hides a dell,
Where swain, or woodman lone,
might dwell;
There's nothing left to fancy's guess,
You see that all is loneliness:
And silence aids – though the steep hills
Send to the lake a thousand rills;
In summer tide, so soft they weep,
The sound but lulls the ear asleep;
Your horse's hoof-tread sounds too rude,
So stilly is the solitude.

WALTER SCOTT, 'ST MARY'S LAKE'

We look to Scotland for all our ideas of civilisation.

VOLTAIRE

I always said that when I met MacDiarmid, I had met a great poet who said 'Och'.

SEAMUS HEANEY ON MEETING HUGH MACDIARMID

Then away to the west – to
the beautiful west!
To the fair city of Glasgow
that I like the best,
Where the river Clyde rolls
on to the sea,
And the lark and the
blackbird whistle with glee.

WILLIAM MCGONAGALL, FROM 'GLASGOW'

Go fetch to me a pint o' wine,
And fill it in a silver tassie;
That I may drink, before I go,
A service to my bonie lassie:
The boat rocks at the pier o' Leith,
Fu' loud the wind blaws frae the Ferry,
The ship rides by the Berwick-law,
And I maun leave my bony Mary.

The trumpets sound, the banners fly,
The glittering spears are ranked ready,
The shouts o' war are heard afar,
The battle closes deep and bloody.
It's not the roar o' sea or shore,
Wad make me langer wish to tarry;
Nor shouts o' war that's heard afar –
It's leaving thee, my bony* Mary!

ROBERT BURNS, 'MY BONY MARY'

*bony – bonnie

33

There is only mist, wind, rain, the cry of the curlew and the slow clouds above damp moorland. That is the real Scotland... that even a stranger learns to love.

H. V. MORTON, *IN SEARCH OF SCOTLAND*

How beautiful is Dunfermline seen from the Ferry Hills, its grand old abbey towering over all, seeming to hallow the city and to lend a charm and dignity to the lowliest tenement... What Benares is to the Hindu, Mecca to the Mohammedan, Jerusalem to the Christian, all that is Dunfermline to me.

ANDREW CARNEGIE, *AN AMERICAN FOUR-IN-HAND IN BRITAIN*

This is a city of shifting light, of changing skies, of sudden vistas. A city so beautiful it breaks the heart again and again.

ALEXANDER MCCALL SMITH ON EDINBURGH

If your words are to be set in stone, then you have to be careful what you say! You have to mean it. And I do mean what I say about this magnificent city, of which I am proud to be a citizen and which will always be my home.

ALEXANDER MCCALL SMITH

I would be very pleased to move to Edinburgh because it is one of my favourite cities in the world... You just feel elated to be walking through the city.

CAROL ANN DUFFY

I think it is a great good on the whole [the generalist democratic approach of Scottish education], because it enables relatively large numbers of people to get – not indeed profound learning, for that is not to be spoken of – but that knowledge which tends to liberalise and make intelligent the mass of our population, more than anything else.

FRANCIS JEFFRAY

[The Highlander has] the exclusive advantage, when halted, of drenching his kilt in the next brook, as well as washing his limbs, and drying both, as it were by constant fanning, without injury to either, but on the contrary feeling clean and comfortable.

ALAN CAMERON OF ERRACHT,
A LETTER TO THE WAR OFFICE

For me I can be well content
To eat my bannock on the bent,
And kitchen't wi' fresh air;
Of lang-kail I can make a feast,
And cantily had up my crest,
And laugh at dishes rare.

ALLAN RAMSAY,
FROM 'THE POET'S WISH: AN ODE'

Why runs thy stream,
O Yarrow, Yarrow red?
Why on thy braes heard
the voice of sorrow?
And why yon melancholeous weids
Hung on the bony birks of Yarrow!

WILLIAM HAMILTON,
FROM 'THE BRAES OF YARROW'

That I, for poor auld Scotland's sake
Some usefu' plan or book could make,
     Or sing a sang at least.
The rough burr-thistle, spreading wide
     Amang the bearded bear,
I turn'd the weeder-clips aside,
     An' spar'd the symbol dear.
     No nation, no station
     My envy e'er could raise:
     A Scot still, but blot still,
     I knew no higher praise.

**ROBERT BURNS, FROM 'THE ANSWER,
TO THE GUIDWIFE OF WAUCHOPE-HOUSE'**

Chivalry! – why, maiden, she is the nurse of pure and high affection – the stay of the oppressed, the redresser of grievances, the curb of the power of the tyrant – Nobility were but an empty name without her, and liberty finds the best protection in her lance and her sword.

WALTER SCOTT, *IVANHOE*

B eautiful as ever, of course
– for nothing can be finer
than the ridge of the Old Town
etched on hot summer azure.

ALEXANDER SMITH ON EDINBURGH,
A SUMMER IN SKYE

Aye, I'm telling ye, happiness is one of the few things in this world that doubles every time you share it with someone else.

HARRY LAUDER

Ye canna recite Burns juist oot o yer heid. If it disnae come fae yer hert and up through yer heid, it's no worth sayin. Because it must touch the hert, because Burns touched the hert a' the time.

WULLIE MORRISON, AYRSHIRE GROCER AND BURNS ENTHUSIAST

The proper drinking of
Scotch whisky is... a
toast to a civilisation.

DAVID DAICHES

A deep shade hung over the road, where some little boys were at play; we expected a dwelling-house of some sort; and when we came nearer, saw three or four thatched huts under the trees, and at the same moment felt that it was a paradise. We had before seen the lake only as one wide plain of water; but here the portion of it which we saw was bounded by a high and steep, heathy and woody island opposite, which did not appear like an island, but the main shore, and framed out a little oblong lake apparently not so broad as Rydale-water, with one small island covered with trees, resembling some of the most beautiful of the holms of Windermere, and only a narrow river's breadth from the shore. This was a place where we should have liked to have lived, and the only one we had seen near Loch Lomond. How delightful to have a little shed concealed under the branches of the fairy island! ... I thought, what a place for William! he might row himself over with twenty strokes of the oars, escaping from the business of the house, and as safe from intruders, with his boat anchored beside him, as if he had locked himself up in the strong tower of a castle. We were unwilling to leave this sweet spot; but it was so simple, and therefore so rememberable, that it seemed almost as if we could have carried it away with us.

DOROTHY WORDSWORTH, *RECOLLECTIONS OF A TOUR MADE IN SCOTLAND, AD 1803*

It is not so much for its beauty that the forest makes a claim upon men's hearts, as for that subtle something, that quality of air that emanates from old trees, that so wonderfully changes and renews a weary spirit.

ROBERT LOUIS STEVENSON, *ESSAYS ON TRAVEL*

At last it comes, the 1st of August, and then – like an arrow from a Tartar's bow, like a bird from its cage, like a lover to his mistress – one is off; and before the wild scarlets of sunset die on the northern sea, one is in the silence of the hills, those eternal sundials that tell the hours to the shepherd, and in one's nostrils is the smell of peat-reek, and in one's throat the flavour of usquebaugh.

ALEXANDER SMITH, *A SUMMER IN SKYE*

Old Strevline, thou stand'st
beauteous on the height,
Amid thy peaceful vales
of every dye,
Amid bewildered waves
of silvery light
That maze the mind and toil
the raptured eye;
Thy distant mountains spiring to the sky,
Seem blended with the
mansions of the blest;
How proudly rise their gilded
points on high
Above the morning cloud
and man's behest!
Like thrones of angels hung upon
the welkin's breast.

For these I love thee!
but I love thee more
For the grey relics of
thy martial towers,
Thy mouldering palaces
and ramparts hoar,
Throned on the granite pile
that grimly lours,
Memorial of the times,
when hostile powers
So often proved thy stedfast
patriot worth.
May every honour wait thy
future hours,
And glad the children of
thy kindred Forth!
I love thy very name, old
bulwark of the North!

James Hogg, from 'Mador of the Moor'

I feel a sort of reverence in going over these scenes in this most beautiful country, which I am proud to call my own, where there was such devoted loyalty to the family of my ancestors – for Stuart blood is in my veins.

QUEEN VICTORIA, JOURNAL ENTRY

For who would leave, unbrib'd,
Hibernia's Land,
Or change the rocks of Scotland
for the Strand?

SAMUEL JOHNSON, FROM 'LONDON'

I hae a good ha house,
a barn and a byre,
A peatstack 'fore the door,
we'll make a rantin fire;
I'll make a rantin fire,
and merry shall we be,
And gin ye winna tak me,
I can let ye be.

ALLAN RAMSAY, *THE GENTLE SHEPHERD*

Fight on, brave knights!
Man dies, but glory lives!
Fight on; death is better than
defeat!

WALTER SCOTT, *IVANHOE*

When we first rade down Ettrick,
Our bridles were ringing,
our hearts were dancing,
The waters were singing, the
sun was glancing,
An' blithely our hearts rang
out thegither,
As we brushed the dew frae
the blooming heather,
When we first rade down Ettrick.

When we next rade down Ettrick,
The day was dying, the
wild birds calling,
The wind was sighing, the
leaves were falling,
An' silent an' weary,
but closer thegither,
We urged our steeds thro'
the faded heather,
When we next rade down Ettrick.

When I last rade down Ettrick,
   The winds were shifting,
   the storm was waking,
   The snow was drifting,
   my heart was breaking,
For we never again were to ride thegither,
In sun or storm on the mountain heather,
   When I last rade down Ettrick.

LADY JOHN SCOTT, 'ETTRICK'

I like to tell people when they ask 'Are you a native born?' 'No sir, I am a Scotsman' and I feel as proud as I am sure every Roman did when it was their boast to say 'I am a Roman citizen'.

ANDREW CARNEGIE

The bagpipe is, perhaps, the only national instrument in Europe. Every other is peculiar to many countries, but the bagpipe to Scotland alone. There in the banquet hall and in the house of mourning it has alike prevailed. It has animated her warriors in battle, and welcomed them back after their toils, to the homes of their love, and the hills of their nativity. Its strains were the first sounded on the ears of infancy, and they are the last to be forgotten in the wanderings of age.

DONALD MACDONALD, *THE HIGHLAND SOCIETY OF SCOTLAND*

We come here with no peaceful intent,
but ready for battle, determined to
avenge our wrongs and set our country
free. Let your masters come and attack
us: we are ready to meet them beard to
beard.

WILLIAM WALLACE

A berdeen impresses the stranger as a city of granite palaces, inhabited by people as definite as their building material.

H. V. MORTON, *IN SEARCH OF SCOTLAND*

This nation must rank among the most enlightened in the universe. Politics, religion and literature have made of Scotland something beyond compare.

CHARLES DE RÉMUSAT

It was quite a pantry: oatcakes, barley scones, flour scones, butter, honey, sweetmeats, cheese, and wine, and spiced whisky, all came out of the deep shelves of this agreeable recess, as did the great key of the dairy: this was often given to one of us to carry to old Mary, the cook, with leave to see her skim and whip the fine rich cream, which Mrs Grant would afterwards pour on a whole pot of jam and give us for luncheon. This dish, under the name of 'bainne briste', or broken milk, is a great favourite wherever it has been introduced.

ELIZABETH GRANT, *MEMOIRS OF A HIGHLAND LADY*

At times I lent him for a game
To north and south and east and west,
But no for lang, he sune cam hame,
For here it was he played the best.

**J. M. BARRIE, FROM 'SCOTLAND'S LAMENT:
A POEM ON THE DEATH OF ROBERT
LOUIS STEVENSON'**

Bonnie lassie, will ye go,
  Will ye go, will ye go;
Bonnie lassie, will ye go
To the birks of Aberfeldy.

ROBERT BURNS,
FROM 'THE BIRKS OF ABERFELDY'

I am one of those who always think it is fun to be in Scotland.

HILAIRE BELLOC

Where ancient Corehouse
hangs above the stream,
And far beneath the tumbling
surges gleam,
Engulphed in crags, the
fretting river raves,
Chafed into foam, resound his
tortured waves:
With giddy heads we view the
dreadful deep,
And cattle snort, and tremble
at the steep,
Where down at once the
foaming waters pour,
And tottering rocks repel the
deafening roar.

John Wilson, from 'Clyde'

O Scotia! my dear,
my native soil!
For whom my warmest
wish to heaven is sent;
Long may thy hardy sons
of rustic toil
Be blest with health, and
peace, and sweet content.

ROBERT BURNS,
FROM 'THE COTTER'S SATURDAY NIGHT'

It's different in Scotland. People who come to readings are more interested in literature, as such.

IRVINE WELSH

I always liked Scotland as an idea, but now, as a reality, I like it far better... and who indeed that has once seen Edinburgh, with its couchant crag-lion, but must see it again in dreams waking or sleeping? My dear Sir, do not think I blaspheme when I tell you that your Great London as compared to Dun-Edin 'mine own romantic town' is as prose compared to poetry, or as a great rumbling, rambling, heavy Epic – compared to a lyric bright, brief, clear and vital as a flash of lightning. You have nothing like Scott's Monument, or, if you had that and all the glories of architecture assembled together, you have nothing like Arthur's Seat, and above all you have not the Scotch National Character – and it is that grand character after all which gives the land its true charm, its true greatness.

CHARLOTTE BRONTË, LETTER TO W. S. WILLIAMS

What butter and whisky will not cure,
there is no cure for.

SCOTTISH PROVERB

Come
Home.

**GEORGE MACDONALD, 'THE SHORTEST AND
SWEETEST OF SONGS'**

This is my country,
The land that begat me,
These windy spaces
Are surely my own.

O Brignall banks are wild
and fair,
And Greta woods are green,
And you may gather
garlands there,
Would grace a summer queen.

WALTER SCOTT, FROM 'BRIGNALL BANKS'

I 'scotched, not killed' the
Scotchman in my blood,
And love the land of
mountain and of flood.

LORD BYRON, FROM *DON JUAN*

Flow gently, sweet Afton, among
thy green braes,
Flow gently, I'll sing thee a song
in thy praise;
My Mary's asleep by thy
murmuring stream,
Flow gently, sweet Afton, disturb
not her dream.

Thou stock-dove, whose echo
resounds thro' the glen,
Ye wild whistling blackbirds in
yon thorny den,
Thou green-crested lapwing, thy
screaming forbear,
I charge you disturb not my
slumbering fair.

How lofty, sweet Afton, thy
neighbouring hills,
Far mark'd with the courses of
clear winding rills;
There daily I wander as noon
rises high,
My flocks and my Mary's sweet
cot in my eye.

How pleasant thy banks and
green valleys below,
Where wild in the woodlands the
primroses blow;
There oft, as mild ev'ning leaps
over the lea,
The sweet-scented birk shades
my Mary and me.

Thy crystal stream, Afton, how
lovely it glides,
And winds by the cot where my
Mary resides,
How wanton thy waters her
snowy feet lave,
As gathering sweet flow, rets she
stems thy clear wave.

Flow gently, sweet Afton, among
thy green braes,
Flow gently, sweet river, the
theme of my lays;
My Mary's asleep by thy
murmuring stream,
Flow gently, sweet Afton, disturb
not her dream.

ROBERT BURNS, 'AFTON WATER'

No father here but would give a son
    For the old country,
And his mother the sword
    would have girded on
    To fight her battles:
Many's the battle that has been won
    By the brave tartans,
        Glenaradale.

But the big-horn'd stag and
    his hinds, we know,
    In the high corries,
And the salmon that swirls
    in the pool below
Where the stream rushes
Are more than the hearts
    of men, and so
We leave thy green valley,
        Glenaradale.

WALTER CHALMERS SMITH, FROM
'GLENARADALE'

What shall we, in half an hour, yield what our forebears maintained with their lives and fortunes for many ages! Are none of the descendants here of those worthy patriots who defended the liberty of their country against all invaders – who assisted the great King Robert Bruce to restore the constitution, and avenge the falsehood of England and usurpation of Baliol? Where are the Douglases and the Campbells?

JAMES DOUGLAS HAMILTON, IN A
PARLIAMENTARY SPEECH OPPOSING
UNION WITH ENGLAND

William Wallace sheds as bright a glory upon his valorous nation as ever was shed upon their country by the greatest men of Greece or Rome.

GIUSEPPE GARIBALDI

Scotsmen are metaphysical and emotional, they are sceptical and mystical, they are romantic and ironic, they are cruel and tender, and full of mirth and despair.

WILLIAM DUNBAR

Of all the small nations of this earth, perhaps only the Ancient Greeks surpass the Scots in their contribution to mankind.

WINSTON CHURCHILL

Away, ye gay landscapes,
ye gardens of roses,
In you let the minions of luxury rove,
Restore me the rocks where the snow-
flake reposes,
Though still they are sacred to
freedom and love.
Yet Caledonia, beloved are thy mountains,
Round their white summits though
elements war,
Though cataracts foam 'stead of
smooth-flowing fountains,
I sigh for the valley of dark Lochnagar.

Ah! there my young footsteps
in infancy wander'd,
My cap was the bonnet, my
cloak was the plaid.
On chieftains long perish'd
my memory ponder'd
As daily I strode through the
pine-cover'd glade.
I sought not my home till the
day's dying glory
Gave place to the rays of the
bright polar star,
For fancy was cheer'd by traditional story
Disclos'd by the natives of dark Lochnagar!

Shades of the dead! Have I not
heard your voices
Rise on the night-rolling breath
of the gale?
Surely the soul of the hero rejoices,
And rides on the wind o'er his
own Highland vale.
Round Lochnagar while the
stormy mist gathers,
Winter presides in his cold icy car.
Clouds there encircle the forms
of my fathers;
They dwell in the tempests of
dark Lochnagar.

LORD BYRON, 'LOCHNAGAR'

H aunting and exasperatingly
lovable.

LEWIS GRASSIC GIBBON ON ABERDEEN

It is a fine thing for you to have a love of the hills, because on the hills you find yourself near grand and beautiful things.

SETON GORDON, LETTER TO ADAM WATSON

Ye Pow'rs, wha mak mankind your care,
And dish them out their bill o' fare,
Auld Scotland wants nae skinking ware
That jaups in luggies;
But, if ye wish her gratefu' prayer
Gie her a haggis!

ROBERT BURNS, FROM 'ADDRESS TO A HAGGIS'

It is one of the best trading towns in Scotland, and that as well in foreign business as in manufacture and home trade... It is exceedingly populous, full of stately houses, and large handsome streets... The inhabitants appear here like gentlemen, as well as men of business, and yet are real merchants too.

DANIEL DEFOE, *A TOUR THRO' THE WHOLE ISLAND OF GREAT BRITAIN*

O how canst thou renounce the
boundless store
Of charms which Nature to her
votary yields!
The warbling woodland, the
resounding shore,
The pomp of groves, and garniture
of fields;
All that the genial ray of morning gilds,
And all that echoes to the song of even,
All that the mountain's sheltering
bosom shields,
And all the dread magnificence of heaven,
O how canst thou renounce and hope
to be forgiven!

James Beattie, *The Minstrel*

As every Scot knows, a gallus besom is a cheeky bitch.

MURIEL GRAY, INTERPRETING 'GALLUS BESOM' AFTER AN ENGLISH TELEVISION COMPANY HAD TRANSLATED IT AS A 'LIVELY LASS'

By a dash of the picturesque, by its display of opulence, and by the romance of its crowded quays the proud... series of docks, which are at once the boast of Dundee, the chief means of its wealth, and the best evidence of its enterprise and taste.

THE TOPOGRAPHICAL, STATISTICAL, AND HISTORICAL GAZETTEER OF SCOTLAND

Scots will tell you that their kinsfolk may be justly regarded as being responsible for many important developments over the years: the telephone – Alexander Graham Bell; Penicillin – Alexander Fleming; TV – John Logie Baird; roads and bridges – Thomas Telford.

PAUL HESLOP

The Scottish Enlightenment embarked on nothing less than a massive reordering of human knowledge.

ARTHUR L. HERMAN

What distinguishes Scottish soccer, perhaps, is the permanent triumph of hope over experience.

CLIFF HANLEY

Having been bred amongst mountains I am always unhappy when in a flat country. Whenever the skirts of the horizon come on a level with myself I feel myself quite uneasy and generally have a headache.

JAMES HOGG, LETTER TO WALTER SCOTT

Firm and erect the
Caledonian stood;
Old was his mutton, and his
claret good.
'Let him drink port!' the
Saxon statesman cried.
He drank the poison, and
his spirit died.

JOHN HOME

The Glasgow invention of square-toed shoes was to enable the Glasgow man to get closer to the bar.

JACK HOUSE

I perceive two things in Scotland of the most fearful omen: ignorance of theological truth, and a readiness to pride themselves in and boast of it.

EDWARD IRVING

O, gin I were where Gadie rins,
Where Gadie rins, where
Gadie rins,
O, gin I were where Gadie rins
By the foot o' Bennachie!

JOHN IMLAH, FROM 'O, GIN I WERE
WHERE GADIE RINS!'

On a fine morning there is not in the whole world a prettier sheet of water than Loch Eishart. Everything about it is wild, beautiful, and lonely… You seem to be sailing out of the nineteenth century away back into the ninth… Over the Loch the Cuchullins rise crested with tumult of golden mists; the shores are green behind; and away out, towards the horizon, the

Island of Rum, ten miles long at the least, shoots up from the flat sea like a pointed flame... Beyond Rum, fifteen miles out yonder, the sea is smooth, and flushed with more varied hues than ever lived on the changing opal – dim azures, tender pinks, sleek emeralds. It is one sheet of mother-of-pearl.

ALEXANDER SMITH, *A SUMMER IN SKYE*

Sheltered from the Atlantic by the huge
breakwater of Cantyre, the Firth of Clyde
is a great natural harbour; its wide mouth
gives a ready entrance in every wind; and
it ends in an estuary that cuts deep into
the land, piercing almost the North Sea.
But the map will not tell all that Nature
has done for us. The Firth swarms with
herring, and the river once swarmed with
salmon: from Ailsa Craig to the Tail of

the Bank the Firth is deep, clean water, without a shoal or a rock: the river has no bar, and it reaches as a tidal creek the edge of a great mineral basin. Nature had done her part that somewhere in our valley a city should one day rise, a great seat of commerce and manufactures.

JAMES MACLEHOSE, *MEMOIRS AND PORTRAITS OF ONE HUNDRED GLASGOW MEN*

There was wind, there was rain,
there was fire on their faces,
When the clans broke the
bayonets and died on the guns,
And 'tis Honour that watches
the desolate places
Where they sleep through the
change of the snows and the suns.

[...]

Where the graves of Clan Chatton
are clustered together,
Where MacGillivray died by the
Well of the Dead,
We stooped to the moorland and
plucked the pale heather

That bloom where the hope of the
Stuart was sped.
And a whisper awoke on the
wilderness, sighing,
Like the voice of the heroes who
battled in vain,
'Not for Tearach alone the red
claymores was plying,
But to bring back the old life that
comes not again.'

ANDREW LANG, FROM 'CULLODEN'

Behold her, single in the field,
　Yon solitary Highland Lass!
Reaping and singing by herself;
　Stop here, or gently pass!
Alone she cuts and binds the grain,
　And sings a melancholy strain;
O listen! for the Vale profound
Is overflowing with the sound.

No Nightingale did ever chaunt
More welcome notes to weary bands
Of travellers in some shady haunt,
    Among Arabian sands:
A voice so thrilling ne'er was heard
In springtime from the Cuckoo-bird,
    Breaking the silence of the seas
    Among the farthest Hebrides.

**WILLIAM WORDSWORTH,
FROM 'THE SOLITARY REAPER'**

I saw a great part of the border country spread out before me and could trace the scenes of those poems and romances which had in a manner bewitched the world.

WASHINGTON IRVING, *ABBOTSFORD AND NEWSTEAD ABBEY*

I could not live anywhere out of Scotland. All my recollections are Scottish, and consequently all my imaginations; and though I thank God that I have as few fixed opinions as any man of my standing, yet all the elements out of which they are made have a certain national cast also.

FRANCIS JEFFRAY, LETTER TO JOHN MURRAY

From the lone shieling of the
misty island
Mountains divide us, and
the waste of seas
Yet still the blood is strong,
the heart is Highland,
And we in dreams behold
the Hebrides!

FROM 'CANADIAN BOAT-SONG'

W hisky. For the gentlemen that like it and for the gentlemen who don't like it, whisky.

JAMES KENNAWAY, *TUNES OF GLORY*

Golf is a thoroughly national game; it is as Scotch as haggis, cockie-leekie, high cheekbones or rowanberry jam.

ANDREW LANG, *LOST LEADERS*

I like Scottish people because they feel very true. They're always level and straight. They get a reputation for being hardened because of it, but I find them to be scrupulously honest people.

RUPERT FRIEND

Sir Robert the Bruce at Bannockburn
Beat the English in every wheel and turn
And made them fly in great dismay
From off the field without delay.

WILLIAM MCGONAGALL,
FROM 'THE BATTLE OF BANNOCKBURN'

The heathery moors slope down to a distant valley. The sun is setting. The sky above the Lammermuirs is red and troubled.

H. V. MORTON, *THE SPLENDOUR OF SCOTLAND*

Up wi' the flowers of Scotland,
The emblems o' the free
Their guardians for a thousand years,
Their guardians still we'll be,
A foe had better brave the de'il
Within his reeky cell,
Than our thistle's purple bonnet,
Or bonny heather bell.

JAMES HOGG, FROM 'THE FLOWERS
OF SCOTLAND'

When death's dark
stream I ferry o'er,
A time that surely
shall come;
In Heaven itself, I'll
ask no more,
Than just a Highland
welcome.

ROBERT BURNS, 'THE HIGHLAND WELCOME'

Alan Macdonald was completely the figure of a gallant Highlander... He had his tartan plaid thrown round him, a large blue bonnet... a bluish philibeg (kilt) and tartan hose. He had jet black hair tied behind, a large stately man, with a steady sensible countenance.

JAMES BOSWELL

I felt I was fighting for Scotland and my truest happiness lies in the fact that I did not let Scotland down.

BENNY LYNCH

As boys we ran up the brae. As men
and women, young and in our prime,
we almost forgot it was there. But the
autumn of life comes, and the brae
grows steeper; then the winter, and
once again we are as the child pausing
apprehensively on the brig. Yet we are no
longer the child; we look now or no new
world at the top, only for a little garden

and a tiny house, and a handloom in the house. It is only a garden of kail and potatoes, but there may be a line of daisies, white and red, on each side of the narrow footpath, and honeysuckle over the door. Life is not always hard, even after backs grow bent, and we know that all braes lead only to the grave.

J. M. BARRIE, *A WINDOW IN THRUMS*

The thing they ca' the stimy o 't.
 I find it ilka where!
Ye 'maist lie deid – an unco shot –
 Anither's ba is there!
Ye canna win into the hole
 However gleg ye be,
And aye, where'er my ba' may row,
 Some limmer stimies me!

ANDREW LANG,
FROM 'A SONG OF LIFE AND GOLF'

S cotland is my country, the nation that shaped me, that taught me my values.

JOHANN LAMONT

Speed bonnie boat like a bird on the wing,
Onward! the sailors cry;
Carry the lad that's born to be king
Over the sea to Skye.

HAROLD BOULTON,
FROM 'THE SKYE BOAT SONG'

And here's a hand, my trusty fiere!*
And gie's a hand o' thine!
And we'll tak a right quid willie-waught*,
For auld lang syne.
For auld lang syne.

ROBERT BURNS, FROM 'AULD LANG SYNE'

*fiere – friend
*quid willie-waught – draught

There's a real emphasis on being witty in Scotland, even in crime novels.

DENISE MINA

With hound and horn o'er mountain wild
Let huntsmen sportive stray,
By winding stream and lonely loch
Let fishers pass the day;
But dearer far, when skies are blue,
Is yon brave icy plain,
Where curlers meet to ply the broom,
And wing the 'channel-stane!'

GEORGE MURRAY, FROM 'THE BROOM AND
CHANNEL-STANE'

Come, a' ye athletes crouse an' keen,
Frae Gallowa' to Aberdeen,
Wha like to loup or put the stane,
Or rin a race,
Come, let the teardrops frae your een
Rin doun your face.

The noble Fleming's breath'd his last!
My hamely muse stands maist aghast
To mark how Fortune's cauldrife blast,
In hapless time,
Has laid him low ere barely past
His manly prime...

At caber-tossing, when the rest
Had traunchled sair an' dune their best,
Then Jamie to the final test
Wi' power advanced –
Fierce as a cyclone in the west –
An' owre in danc'd!

JAMES KENNEDY, FROM 'ELEGY ON THE DEATH OF JAMES FLEMING, THE SCOTTISH ATHLETE'

In days when mankind
were but callans;
At grammar, logic an'
sic talents,
They took nae pains their
speech to balance,
Or rules to gie;
But spak their thoughts in
plain, braid Lallans,
Like you or me.

ROBERT BURNS,
FROM 'TO W. SIMPSON, OCHILTREE'

A! Freedom is ane nobil thing!
Freedom makis man to have liking,
Freedom all solace to man givis:
He livis at ease that freely livis!
A nobil hart may hae naen ease,
Na ellis nocht that may him pleise,
Gif freedom failye; for free liking
Is yairnit owre all other thing.

JOHN BARBOUR, FROM 'THE BRUS'

Mr Watson, come here, I want to see you.

ALEXANDER GRAHAM BELL'S FIRST WORDS DOWN THE TELEPHONE, TO HIS ASSISTANT

Beautiful town of Montrose, near by
the seaside,
With your fine shops and streets so wide,
'Tis health for the people that in you reside,
Because they do inhale the pure
fragrant air,
Emanating from the sea waves and
shrubberies growing there;
And the inhabitants of Montrose ought
to feel gay,
Because it is one of the bonniest towns
in Scotland at the present day.

WILLIAM MCGONAGALL, FROM 'MONTROSE'

Our principal writers have nearly all been fortunate in escaping regular education.

HUGH MACDIARMID

We shall never learn to feel and respect our real calling and destiny, unless we have taught ourselves to consider everything as moonshine, compared with the education of the heart.

WALTER SCOTT, LETTER TO HIS SON-IN-LAW

But it is in June, I think, that the mountain charm is most intoxicating. The airs are lightsome. The hill-mists are seldom heavy, and only on south-wind mornings do the lovely grey-white vapours linger among the climbing corries and overhanging scarps. Many of the slopes are blue, aerially delicate, from the incalculable myriad host of the bluebells. The green of the bracken is more wonderful than at any other time... Everything is alive in joy. The young broods exult. The air is vibrant with the eddies of many wings, great and small. The shadow-grass sways with the passage of the shrewmouse or the wing's breath of the darting swallow. The stillest pool quivers, for among the shadows of breathless reeds the phantom javelin of the dragonfly whirls for a second from silence to silence.

FIONA MACLEOD, *THE SILENCE OF AMOR*

But I am half a Scot by
birth, and bred
A whole one, and my heart
flies to my head
As Auld Lang Syne
brings Scotland, one and all
Scotch plaids, Scotch snoods,
the blue hills, and clear streams,
The Dee, the Don, Balgounie's
Brig's black wall,
All my boy feelings, all
my gentler dreams
Of what I then dreamt, clothed
in their own pall,
Like Banqo's offspring.
Floating past me seems
My childhood in this
childishness of mine;
I care not – 'tis a glimpse of
Auld Lang Syne.

LORD BYRON, FROM *DON JUAN*

The best food in the world comes from Scotland, in part at least, because Scotland is the last wilderness area in Europe.

CLAIRE MACDONALD

Having little else to cultivate, they cultivated the intellect. The export of brains came to be their chief item of commerce.

STEPHEN LEACOCK ON THE SCOTS

There is nothing the Scots like better to hear than abuse of the English.

POPE PIUS II

You've forgotten the grandest moral attribute of a Scotsman, Maggie, that he'll do nothing which might damage his career.

J. M. BARRIE, *WHAT EVERY WOMAN KNOWS*

O ye'll tak' the high road, and
I'll tak' the low road,
And I'll be in Scotland afore ye,
But me and my true love will
never meet again,
On the bonnie, bonnie banks o'
Loch Lomond.

FROM 'THE BONNIE BANKS O' LOCH LOMOND'

Here's tae us; wha's like us?
Gey few, and they're a' deid.

SCOTTISH TOAST

Scotland is first and foremost home... What I treasure is the light, the space, the rain, and above all, the unsentimental friendship of the people.

SHEENA MCDONALD

But after we had journeyed about six miles a beautiful scene opened upon us. The morning had been gloomy, and at this time the sun shone out, scattering the clouds. We looked right down the lake, that was covered with streams of dazzling sunshine, which revealed the indentings of the dark shores. On a bold promontory, on the same side of the loch where we were, stood an old castle, an irregular tall building, not without majesty; and beyond, with leagues of water between, our eyes settled upon the island of Mull, a high mountain, green in the sunshine, and overcast with clouds, – an object as inviting to the fancy as the evening sky in the west, and though of a terrestrial green, almost as visionary. We saw that it was an island of the seas but were unacquainted with its name; it was of a gem-like colour, and as soft as the sky. The shores of Loch Etive, in their moorish, rocky wildness, their earthly bareness, as they lay in length before us, produced a contrast which, with the pure sea, the brilliant sunshine, the long distance, contributed to the aërial and romantic power with which the mountain island was invested.

DOROTHY WORDSWORTH, *RECOLLECTIONS OF A TOUR MADE IN SCOTLAND, AD 1803*

Where the pools are bright and deep
Where the grey trout lies asleep,
Up the river and o'er the lea
That's the way for Billy and me.

JAMES HOGG, FROM 'A BOY'S SONG'

In the highlands, in the
country places,
Where the old plain men
have rosy faces.

ROBERT LOUIS STEVENSON,
FROM 'IN THE HIGHLANDS'

Burns for me has always been one of the greatest love poets.

CAROL ANN DUFFY

When the sheep are in the fauld, when
the cows come hame,
When a' the weary world to quiet rest
are gane,
The woes of my heart fa' in showers
frae my ee,
Unken'd by my gudeman, who soundly
sleeps by me.

LADY ANNE LINDSAY, FROM 'AULD ROBIN GRAY'

She saw a sun on a summer sky,
And clouds of amber sailing bye;
A lovely land beneath her lay,
And that land had glens and
mountains grey;
And that land had values and hoary piles;
And marled seas, and a thousand isles;
Its fields were speckled, its forests green,
And its lakes were all of a dazzling sheen.

[...]

She saw the corn wave on the vale,
She saw the deer run down the dale;
She saw the plaid and the broad claymore,
And the brows that the badge of
freedom bore;
And she thought she had seen the
land before.

JAMES HOGG, FROM 'KILMENY'

Love of the land, of its proud capital city, of its country places, and islands remote and mysterious, is a strong vein in the Scot. He is the son of a hundred generations of warriors.

W. H. HAMILTON

Farewell to the Highlands,
farewell to the North –
The birth place of Valour, the
country of Worth:
Wherever I wander,
wherever I rove,
The hills of the Highlands
for ever I love.

ROBERT BURNS,
FROM 'MY HEART'S IN THE HIGHLANDS'

If you're interested in finding out more about our books, find us on Facebook at **Summersdale Publishers** and follow us on Twitter at **@Summersdale**.

www.summersdale.com